Decodable

```
MW01137642
```

Scott Foresman

Editorial Offices: Glenview, Illinois • New York, New York
Sales Offices: Reading, Massachusetts • Duluth, Georgia
Glenview, Illinois • Carrollton, Texas • Menlo Park, California

Printed in the United States of America

ISBN 0-673-65181-9

3 4 5 6 7 8 9 10 - BISF - 06 05 04 03 02 01 00

Contents

3

4

Stars

by Maggie Bridger
illustrated by Tom Barrett

The night sky is dark.
We can see lots and lots of stars!
We can wish on these stars.
We can study them.

We can see stars closely.
We work hard.
It is fun to study stars.

Stay up at night.
See the night sky.
See the stars.

This yard has too much light.
Stars can hardly be seen.
Stars shine dimly.

Find a dark spot.

Try a park.

Stars can be seen much better.

Start looking at stars nightly.
Start looking weekly.
Star watching can be fun!

Stars seem small.
Stars are really big.
Some stars are as big as the sun.
Stars are just far, far away.

Stars seem to spin slowly.
Stars really spin quickly.

A few stars have names.
We can read all about stars.
We can see them on star charts.
We can read maps of the stars.

We can map the night sky.
Mark the stars you see.

We can help study the stars.
Start now!
Look up at the night sky.

Phonics Skill _r_-Controlled _ar_: dark, stars, hard, yard, hardly, park, start, star, are, far, charts, mark

Phonics Skill Suffix _-ly_: closely, hardly, dimly, nightly, weekly, really, slowly, quickly

Spelling Words: far, star, dark, yard, start

Fox and Stork

retold by Myka-Lynne Sokoloff
illustrated by Marvin Glass

"Mine," said Fox.
Stork nodded.

"Hot or cold?" asked Fox.

Stork liked cold meals.

"Cold is fine," said Stork.

"Well, we will see," said Fox.

Fox lived up north. He made
a dish he liked to eat. He made
hot pork for Stork and himself.

Fox ate and ate and ate.
Eating was hard for Stork.
The meal was hot. The
plate was flat. Stork's beak did
not fit! She did not eat a bit!

"I am full," said Fox. He
licked his lips.

Stork did not like eating
with Fox.

"Hot or cold?" asked Stork.

"Hot is fine," said Fox.

"Well, we will see," said Stork.

Fox went to Stork's home.
Fox started eating. His nose
did not fit. The meal was not
hot. Fox was too short. Fox did
not eat at all!

Stork ate and ate and ate
from the jar.

Fox did not like eating
with Stork.

"Fox," says Stork. "This is a treat for you. I hope this teaches you to treat me as well as you want to be treated."

Phonics Skill *r*-Controlled *or:* *Stork, or, north, pork, for, Stork's, short*

Phonics Skill Inflected Endings -s, -es, -ed, -ing: *nodded, asked, liked, lived, licked, eating, started, says, teaches, treated*

Spelling Words: *for, or, short*

On Mark's Farm

REVIEW

by Jeanine Bermes
illustrated by John Dyess

"Get in my blue car," Dad said. "We are going for a short car ride."

"We are going to Mark's farm," Mom said. "We want to get to Mark's farm quickly."

On Mark's farm, we will
see his big red barn. Ten
chicks were born this morning
inside Mark's big red barn.

On Mark's farm, we will
see six black kittens playing
in his barnyard. Six black
kittens like to chase small
white mice.

On Mark's farm, we will
see his corn growing very
tall. We hope that his goats
are not eating his corn!

On Mark's farm, we will
see his trees. A bug slowly
lands on a small green leaf.

On Mark's farm, we hope it will not rain. We forgot to bring raincoats! We can hardly wait to get to Mark's farm.

On Mark's farm, we will see his garden. He is growing lots of plants in his farmyard garden. We will look for big bugs in his garden.

On Mark's farm, we will
see big white sheep. Bart
brushes the fuzzy sheep.

On Mark's farm, we will
see five pink pigs playing in
the pigpen. We will feed
Mark's pigs lots of corn.

On Mark's farm, we will
run and play in the bright
yellow sunshine.

On Mark's farm, Dad will park his blue car in Mark's yard. We will have fun on Mark's farm.

Phonics Skill *r*-Controlled *ar:* car, Mark's, farm, barn, barnyard, garden, farmyard, Bart, park, yard

Phonics Skill *r*-Controlled *or:* for, short, born, morning, corn

Phonics Skill Suffix *-ly:* quickly, slowly, hardly

Phonics Skill Inflected Endings *-s, -es, -ed, -ing:* going, playing, growing, lands, eating, brushes

Spelling Words: car, yard, for, short, born

Gert and That Big Dust Storm

by Deborah Eaton
illustrated by Drew-Brook-Cormack

Gert is some girl.

She rides. She ropes. She does it all.

Gert is the best in the West!

One night Gert needed a bright
light. She just roped the brightest
light in the night sky.

That girl was sweeter than candy.
One day she met up with a
bobcat. My, my! He was mean!
Gert looked at that bobcat. Gert
smiled at him. She made that cat
start to purr!

Gert rode anything. Yes, sir!
She did! She did not let go.
One time she rode a huge
dust storm.

It was hotter than hot. We had not seen a drop of rain. Then a big storm blew in. It was darker than night.

That storm started to turn.
It started to whirl and swirl.
Faster and faster it went!

Dirt flew. Trees hugged each other. Corn turned inside out. Thirty crows blew away. A herd of goats flew off.

Which way might the storm turn next?

"Gert!" I yelled.

Quick as a wink, there she was.
Gert went right up to that storm.
She jumped right on that storm.

Up, up, up she flew. The
storm twisted. It turned
under her, but Gert held on.
"Yippee!" she yelled.
Gert had a lot of fun with
that storm!

Gert rode that storm. She sent
it on its way. Thanks to Gert, no
one got hurt.

First she made it dig a hole. We
all got a brand new well!

Yes, sir! That Gert is
some girl!

Phonics Skill r-Controlled *er, ir, ur:* *Gert, girl, purr, sir, turn, whirl, swirl, dirt, turned, thirty, herd, her hurt, first*

Phonics Skill Comparative Endings *-er* and *-est:* *brightest, sweeter, hotter, darker, faster*

Spelling Words: *her, turn, hurt, girl, first*

Funny Clowns

by Max Greene
illustrated by John Manders

Who makes funny faces?
Who wins silly races? Who
makes us smile? Clowns!

How do clowns get so funny?
Clowns use makeup and big
red noses.

Clowns dress in huge, baggy
pants and big, bright shirts.

That clown is up, and that
clown is down.

When clowns act silly, crowds
yell and laugh.

Clowns are so funny crowds
hardly see men helping the
clowns.

Clowns play tricks on clowns
and fans.

This silly clown has a tricky
can. Fake snakes pop up at a fan.

See this clown with his tall,
tall crown? He rides his bike up
and down. Going too fast, he hits
a pole. Now his wheel has a big
dent, and he can't go.

This clown's home is filling with smoke. Clown firemen run to save the clown. When she jumps, she crashes down.

This clown can't see his rabbit.
He checks his brown cape.
He shakes his big hat. Where is
his rabbit? It's eating dinner!

Two clowns race. Did one
clown use up all his gas?
Which clown will win?

This clown likes fishing.
He drops his line down in the tub.
Then he feels a big tug.
He catches a shark!
Run for your life, clown!

See these clowns?
All of them ride in one car.
Ten big clowns in one small car!
Now that's a crowd!

All the clowns take bows or tip
hats. It's time to stop being silly.
They all had fun. Did you?

Phonics Skill Vowel Diphthong *ow /ou/*: *clowns, how, down, crowds, clown, crown, now, clown's, brown, crowd, bows*

Phonics Skill Medial Consonants (two-syllable words): *funny, silly, baggy, hardly, tricky, rabbit, dinner*

Spelling Words: *how, now, down, brown, clown*

Sir Bird

REVIEW

by Nathaniel Morgan
illustrated by Jane Kendall

As cows first stir
And kittens start to purr
Let's go down this way
As night turns to day.

In a town named Bower
Up this high stone tower
Sat a girl in red
On her softest bed.

Then this bird all brown
Came whirling down
With a funny frown
And a tiny crown.

Now, this bird was hurt
And all full of dirt.

Sir Bird was his name.
Singing was his game.

This girl had first aid.
Her plan was a trade.
This singer would sing
For a clean, set wing.

Notes sweeter than sweet
Float down on the street.

When his singing has ended,
Sir Bird is all mended.

Now there is no frown
On Sir Bird's brow all brown.
Now this sweet, sweet miss
On his cheek plants a kiss.

Will he turn and whirl
And surprise this girl?
Will he turn into her king?

No such thing!

**Phonics Skill *r*-Controlled *er, ir, ur:* *first, stir, purr, turns, girl, her, bird, whirling, hurt, dirt, Sir, turn, whirl*

Phonics Skill Comparative Endings *-er, -est:* *softest, sweeter*

Phonics Skill Vowel Diphthong *ow /ou/:* *cows, down, town, Bower, tower, brown, frown, crown, now, brow*

Phonics Skill Medial Consonants (two-syllable words): *funny, kittens, surprise*

Spelling Words: *her, turn, hurt, girl, first, bird, now, town, down, brown*

Happy Hound

by Carolyn Kelly
illustrated by Eldon Doty

Hound did not feel happy.
He had a big house, but he
felt lonely.

Hound had a bright idea! He
knew how to make life better.
Hound got brushes and paints to
make a painting.

Hound needed a few pals. He painted a picture. It showed a dog pound. Hound painted lots of dogs and a puppy.

Hound jumped into the
painting. He let out all the dogs
and the puppy.

The dogs went home with
Hound. Now he was not lonely.
He had lots of pals. Hound
was happy!

Brown dog was a grouch. He liked sleeping on the couch. He liked sleeping in the sun. He pouted when clouds hid the sun.

The spotted dog barked too
much. The puppy cried. He cried
louder and louder.

"Ouch!" shouted Hound.
"That sound hurts."

Then Hound had an idea! He
got out brushes and paints. He
painted grass and trees. Hound
jumped into his painting.

Hound now ran and ran.
He played in the grass. Then
Hound curled up to rest. Hound
felt like a happy dog! Best of all,
he can see his pals when he
wishes.

Phonics Skill Vowel Diphthong *ou* /ou/: *Hound, house, pound, out, grouch, couch, pouted, clouds, louder, ouch, shouted, sound*

Phonics Skill Medial Consonants (two-syllable words): *happy, better, picture, puppy*

Spelling Words: *happy, puppy, better*

Roy's Camping Trip

by Betsy Franco
illustrated by Amy Wummer

"School starts in three days.
Let's go camping!" said Mom.

"Can our dog Roy join us?"
asked Kim.

"Yes," said Mom.

We all helped pack the
car. Troy got his toys. Kim
got foil and oil. Joy got
sleeping bags.

It was getting late. We didn't
see the campground. Joy found
a map. She pointed to it.

"There's one spot left just for us," said Kim. "This spot isn't big, but we'll fit. It will not spoil our trip!"

We made a campfire. We
made popcorn on the fire. Roy
started digging in the soil.

Kim yelled, "Stop, Roy! You
cannot spoil our trip!"

Troy wouldn't sleep.
"Noise is fine," Mom said.
"That noise is outside. Noise
will not spoil our trip!"

In the morning, we made a
fire outside. We boiled eggs and
made toast on foil.

"These boiled eggs taste fine.
This toast is burned," said Joy,
"but the toast isn't that bad. It
will not spoil our trip!"

Kim said, "Roy enjoys this
toast! He enjoys these eggs!
Good boy, Roy."

Then it started raining.

"We didn't bring raincoats,"
said Mom, "but rain will not
spoil our trip!"

Then it was time to drive
home. Joy pointed to a rainbow.
She shouted, "We had fun!
Not one thing spoiled our trip!"

Phonics Skill Vowel Diphthongs *oi, oy*: *Roy, join, Troy, toys, foil, oil, Joy, pointed, spoil, soil, noise, boiled, enjoys, boy*

Phonics Skill Multisyllabic Words (compounds, contractions, and inflected endings): *camping, sleeping, getting, didn't, campground, pointed, isn't, campfire, popcorn, started, digging, cannot, wouldn't, outside, raincoats, rainbow, shouted, raining*

Spelling Words: *cannot, outside, popcorn*

Miss Pound's Popcorn

REVIEW

by Lindy Lynk
illustrated by Meryl Treatner

Roy and Joy planned to
go see Miss Pound. She lives
down the block. Roy and Joy
ride bikes to her house on
nice days. It was sunny
outside, so Roy and Joy
rode away.

Something seemed funny
at Miss Pound's house. Roy
and Joy tapped on her
window and peeked inside.

"Where is Miss Pound?"
Roy and Joy asked.

"Don't pout. Let's do
something," said Roy.
"Let's shout for Miss Pound.
Maybe she's outside in her
backyard."

"Miss Pound, it's Roy and Joy! We came to visit!" called Roy.

"Miss Pound isn't home, Roy," said Joy. "I feel silly shouting like this."

Just then Miss Pound's
voice came from inside.
"Wait! Don't go home!
I'm in the kitchen. I'll be out
right away."

Miss Pound came outside
and hugged Roy and Joy.
She seemed happy. She
clapped her hands and
smiled. "Wait outside, Roy
and Joy," said Miss Pound.

Roy and Joy sat on the steps. Miss Pound sneaked back inside. Roy and Joy were puzzled.

"Miss Pound is being so silly. Is she hiding something inside?" asked Roy.

Just then Miss Pound came
outside. She had a noisy little
puppy in her arms. It was
fluffy and white. Miss Pound
said, "Roy and Joy, meet
Popcorn, my new puppy."

Popcorn jumped to the ground. She licked Roy, and then she licked Joy. She ran around and around.

"She is a happy puppy, and she likes to play. She needs playmates just like you, Roy and Joy," said Miss Pound.

Phonics Skill Vowel Diphthong *ou:* *Pound, house, outside, Pound's, pout, shout, shouting, ground, out, around*

Phonics Skill Medial Consonants: *sunny, away, funny, window, visit, silly, kitchen, puzzled, happy, little, puppy, fluffy*

Phonics Skill Vowel Diphthongs *oi, oy:* *Roy, Joy, voice, noisy*

Phonics Skill Decoding Multisyllabic Words (Compounds): *outside, something, inside, backyard, Popcorn, playmates*

Spelling Words: *happy, little, puppy, outside, something, popcorn*